RAILWAY HISTORY IN PICTURES
THE WEST COUNTRY

GW 4700 class 2-8-0 No 4701 climbing out of Goodrington with a Paddington to Kingswear express

RAILWAY HISTORY IN PICTURES

The West Country

R. C. RILEY

DAVID & CHARLES : NEWTON ABBOT

ISBN 0 7153 5479 5

Set in 10 on 12pt Plantin
and printed in Great Britain
by W J Holman Limited Dawlish
for David & Charles (Publishers) Limited
South Devon House Newton Abbot Devon

CONTENTS

INTRODUCTION

Before the motor age reached its present intensity there were many who recalled West Country railways as giving them their first glimpse of the sea when holiday-bound. Indeed in the years following World War II when holidays with pay became more widespread the coastal lines of the west enjoyed a greater volume of traffic than ever before. On a Saturday in high summer the number of trains passing over the double track between Taunton and Newton Abbot had to be seen to be believed, and the resources of engines and carriages were strained to their utmost. But that was before Dr Beeching, who decreed that it was uneconomic to use carriages or railway lines to capacity for only a few months in the year. Many resorts which owed their growth to the railway lost their rail connections—the fate of others is in the balance. The rural branches, whose opening had been the cause of great celebration, passed into oblivion almost unnoticed.

The holiday industry was unknown when railways originated in the west. Other industries predominated, copper and tin mining, granite quarries, clay pits and coal mines, and several were served by early tramways of assorted gauges. Most of these were already in decline before the advent of the main line railway, which brought its own problem of gauges. The talented engineer, Isambard Kingdom Brunel, championed the broad gauge of 7ft, and indeed it had its virtues, but the GWR line from London to Bristol was not opened until 1841, by which time the gauge question elsewhere had been settled and other lines built up and down the country were of 4ft 8½in gauge. As the railway system grew and broad and standard gauge lines met, trans-shipment delays became intolerable and on Friday, 20 May 1892 the last broad gauge Cornishman drew out of Paddington, appropriately hauled by **Great Western**. Crowds lined the route to cheer its passing, and there followed the remarkable feat of conversion that enabled Sunday night's mail train to run through to Penzance on the newly laid standard gauge track.

These and other events in the history of West Country railways are worth recording and provide ample evidence of the important part played by the area in the wider story of the whole system of railways in Britain.

Hilaire Belloc once observed that there was 'nothing which compared with creative writing for taking it out of a man'. Nevertheless, the compilation of this book has largely been a labour of love, and as one whose daily round involves a train journey through South London suburbs, but who spends part of his holidays each year in the west it seems particularly apt to include in these pages Bernard Moore's verse 'Travelling' extracted from *A Cornish Chorus* (p63).

R. C. Riley
Summer 1971

TRIBUTE TO AN ENGINEER

Undoubtedly the best known name in the annals of West Country railway history is that of Isambard Kingdom Brunel, 1806-59. He was a gifted, if somewhat erratic engineer, and today is better remembered than Joseph Locke, engineer responsible for construction of the London & South Western Railway. As a railway engineer Locke was second only to Robert Stephenson. Brunel, on the other hand, was a man of many parts and railway engineering was only one of his fields of activity. His name remains inscribed on the famous Royal Albert Bridge, linking the railways of Devon and Cornwall and it has been carried by locomotives and ships.

EARLY RAILWAYS AND TRAMWAYS

Long before the coming of main line railways there were primitive plateways or tramways for the conveyance of the output of local industrial activity. The Combe Down Railway was a very early example, a wooden wagonway laid in 1730 to convey stone from Ralph Allen's quarries near his Prior Park estate to the River Avon near Bath. This scene drawn by Anthony Walker in 1750 is the earliest known railway print.

This vehicle, preserved by Holman Brothers in their Camborne museum and thought to be the oldest railway carriage in the country, was originally used to convey directors and officials of the mineral tramroad from Poldice to Portreath Harbour. Opened about 1812 the line had a life of just over fifty years until closure of the Poldice copper mine brought its purpose to an end. The carriage has flangeless cast iron wheels for use on the L shaped plate rails.

The Haytor Granite Tramway was unusual in that its track was cut from the local stone. Opened in 1820, its construction may have been hastened by the need for Haytor granite in the rebuilding of London Bridge completed in 1825. The line was disused by 1858 since traffic had to be doubly transferred, from wagon to canal barge at Ventiford, from barge to coaster at Teignmouth. At the quarry end of the line some granite pointwork survives; here the line is seen threading Yarner Woods, north of Bovey Tracey.

Earliest railway in Dorset was Benjamin Fayle's Middlebere Plateway of 1806 built to convey ball clay from pits near Norden for loading into barges at Middlebere wharf and thence to Poole Harbour. The earliest Dorset line authorised by Act of Parliament was the Portland Railway, incorporated in 1825 and opened the following year. Horses were used for haulage of the stone wagons at the top and bottom of a steep cable-operated incline. From 1865 the main line companies had a footing in the island with the opening of the Weymouth & Portland Railway, jointly leased and worked by the GWR and SR.

Horses haul a load of stone to Castletown Pier for shipment, with the incline visible in the background Empty wagons stand in the siding at right (above).

Trans-shipment sidings at Castletown, with Portland Railway wagons in the centre and shipping faintly to be seen at left. The Portland Railway survived until 1939, probably because of its non-standard gauge, 4ft 6in (below).

EVOLUTION OF THE GWR

Most important place in the history of railways of the West Country is Bristol for the Great Western was first conceived by merchants of that city and its line from London to Bristol was opened throughout in 1841. The rapid expansion of the GWR elsewhere is not the concern of this book, but it was associated with several other railway companies which continued the main line westwards and were later to be absorbed in the parent system. Notable among these were the Bristol & Exeter Railway, which fulfilled its objectives by degrees between 1841 and 1844, the South Devon Railway which reached Plymouth in 1849 and the Cornwall Railway which ten years later continued the line to Truro, where it met the track of the West Cornwall Railway already open to Penzance. These companies all shared the services of Isambard Kingdom Brunel and, with the exception originally of the West Cornwall Railway, were built to the 7ft 0in gauge he favoured.

Bourne's engraving of the original GWR station at Bristol with Brunel's beautifully designed roof, once described as 'the wooden train hall at its best'. The tracks were removed in recent years and the building is now used to provide additional car parking facilities.

The Bristol scene in 1876—at right the GWR station, at left the B&ER wooden train shed, architecturally less interesting. In the background the B&ER office building which continues to provide railway office accommodaton.

To most travellers that part of the line between Exeter and Newton Abbot which skirts the sea is the best known of all lines in the west. It got off to a bad start for the South Devon Railway favoured atmospheric traction and initially Brunel was confident of its success. The system required stationary engines every few miles to pump the air from a continuous iron pipe laid between the rails. Each train was headed by a piston carriage, from which a rod fitted into a hinged slot in the atmospheric pipe. This rod was connected to a piston inside the pipe and the train propelled by the admission of air behind the piston forcing it towards the vacuum in front. The system was beset with difficulties and survived for less than a year, steam locomotives taking over the working of all SDR trains in September 1848. Atmospheric pipes were put to other uses, at left for example, as a surface water drain at Paignton. The early view of Dawlish below shows at right the former atmospheric pumping station with its distinctive Italianate tower, a disguised chimney. By this time, of course, the atmospheric pipes had been removed and the distinctive bridge-type rail used in broad gauge days can clearly be seen. Note the old crossbar signal, while an SDR saddle tank on a down passenger train pauses in the station.

By the 1860s the broad gauge was proving to be a doubtful blessing. Not only was the gauge different from that of neighbouring railways, but also from other sections of the GWR. Delays caused by the trans-shipment of freight were building up and traders were clamouring for the extension of the standard gauge to overcome this. The decision to alter the gauge was taken in 1866 and two years later the first conversions took place. In 1874 a few West Country lines in Dorset and Somerset were converted but otherwise the GWR route to the west remained broad gauge until its final disappearance in 1892.

The last down broad gauge train at Truro, in charge of 0-6-0 tank 1256 and 0-4-4 tank 3557. These engines were designed as 'convertibles' and were later modified for standard gauge use (above).

A contemporary drawing shows the gauge conversion in progress at Saltash, May 1892 (below).

(Above) A view said to be the first up standard gauge train leaving Plymouth Millbay on Monday, 23 May 1892, in charge of a '3521' class 0-4-4T. There is abundant evidence of discarded timbers beside the tracks. Subsequently in 1894, the GWR adopted bullhead rail as its future standard and the old bridge rails on longitudinal timbers were gradually replaced.

(Opposite below) Broad gauge engines pause at Chippenham, 21 May 1892, en route from the West to Swindon. Leading is Dean 'Convertible' 2-2-2 3024 followed by SDR 4-4-0ST **Sol,** GWR 2-4-0STs **Pollux** and **Melling** and an 0-6-0ST.

Permanent way work in progress at the west end of Taunton station in July 1895 clearly showing the bridge rails still in position. Main line platforms were being extended and bay platforms put in for use by branch trains to Barnstaple or Minehead. The timber built engine shed at right was later demolished and replaced by a brick built roundhouse type shed. There are a few onlookers, including a specially privileged little girl, but most of those posing for the photographer are gangers or labourers, the bowler hat being the predominant form of headgear.

The main line at the turn of the century. A Paddington—Plymouth express passing Uphill Junction, with the Weston-super-Mare loop line coming in at the left. The train of clerestory coaches is in charge of one of the elegant Dean Singles built between 1892 and 1899. Although successful they were soon replaced by larger engines and all were withdrawn by 1915. The engine here is 3060 **Warlock.**

'Bulldog' 4-4-0 3340 **Marazion,** later 3328, approaches Penzance across the viaduct, which was replaced by stone embankment in 1921.

In 1906 the Castle Cary—Taunton line was opened throughout reducing the mileage between London and the West by twenty miles as compared with the former route via Bristol. Four years earlier Churchward had taken over as Mechanical Engineer and this 1909 photograph shows the transformed GWR express of the twentieth century, a 4-6-0 locomotive with eight Dreadnought type coaches. The train is the Cornish Riviera Limited, introduced on 18 July 1904, and is seen leaving Whiteball Tunnel. 'Saint' Class 4-6-0 173 **Robins Bolitho** is in charge for the non-stop run between Paddington and Plymouth, which then took 4hr 10min via Castle Cary.

The same train fifteen years later. 'Star' Class 4-6-0 4042 **Prince Albert** heads the up Riviera near Teignmouth.

EVOLUTION OF THE LSWR

The LSWR's first access to the West Country was by means of the Southampton and Dorchester Railway, opened in 1847 and following a circuitous route through Ringwood, Wimborne and Wareham. The Dorchester station was sited with a view to westward extension to Exeter, but although such a line was authorised it was never built, and in 1857 the new GWR Yeovil—Weymouth line cut across the intended route; between Dorchester and Weymouth the line was a joint GWR/LSWR concern. Next LSWR penetration was by means of the Salisbury & Yeovil Railway, opened by degrees in 1859-60 and extended to reach Exeter in the latter year. Although the LSWR route from London to Exeter was twenty miles shorter than the old GWR route via Bristol it was more adversely graded, particularly west of Salisbury.

This contemporary engraving shows the first train at Dorchester in 1847 viewed from Maumbury Rings, a famous prehistoric earthwork used in Roman times as an ampitheatre. Local preservationists fought successfully against the breach of this by the railway, and LSWR trains had to curve round it to join the GWR's Wilts, Somerset and Weymouth line.

A typical LSWR station scene of the 1890s with a Beattie 2-4-0 pausing at Parkstone with an up Weymouth stopping train. The engine is one of a successful class built between 1869 and 1875, as rebuilt by Adams.

Although a forward leap in time, this 1954 photograph of Dorchester shows the awkward legacy of its having been designed as a terminal station. The building at right is the original station (centre opposite), the wooden train shed having been removed in the 1930s. The down platform at left was provided in 1879, but until 1970 up trains had to run ahead and then reverse into the up platform. 'King Arthur' 4-6-0 30739 **King Leodegrance** was at the head of the 2.20pm Weymouth—Andover Junction train made up of LSWR non-corridor stock.

In the far west a curious acquisition by the LSWR in 1845 was the Bodmin & Wadebridge Railway, Cornwall's first locomotive line dating back to 1834. It was not connected with the rest of the LSWR system until 1895. Two years earlier a Beattie 2-4-0 tank was shipped to Wadebridge to replace a life-expired four coupled saddle tank, and remarkably the last three survivors of this once numerous Beattie class were used on the B&WR's Wenford Bridge mineral branch from 1898 to 1962. This 1888 view shows some of the original B&W vehicles, two of which survive in Clapham Museum.

Barnstaple Junction in broad gauge days. The line from Crediton opened in 1854 and was worked by the contractor, Brassey, whose 2-2-2 **Tite** is shown. The LSWR acquired the line in 1865 and after some years of mixed gauge working it became wholly standard gauge in 1877.

Railway politics were dominant in the West Country in the 1840s, the period of the railway mania, with intense competition between the GWR and LSWR. In the course of this the LSWR secured control of the Exeter & Crediton Railway by dishonest tactics. The 1846 Regulation of Gauge Act laid down that future lines were to be of standard gauge except where the Board of Trade authorised extension of existing broad gauge lines. Before LSWR intervention in E&C affairs the line was to be leased to the broad gauge Bristol & Exeter Railway. Because the gauge commissioners disapproved of the LSWR's handling of the affair they ruled that the E&C must be broad gauge. As such it was operated by the B&E from 1851 to 1862. in which year the LSWR acquired the lease, after which it was converted to mixed gauge. The 1880 photograph above shows Crediton in mixed gauge days with Beattie 2-4-0 tank 181 in charge of a North Devon train. The 1892 view below shows the wide gap between tracks so familiar on former GWR broad gauge lines but unusual on the LSWR. Note, too, the shunting horse, once a familiar feature of the railway scene.

The LSWR's first access to Plymouth in 1876 was over the GWR's Tavistock and Launceston branch by means of mixed gauge rails running southwards from Lydford to Marsh Mills to a terminus at Devonport. Since the GWR branch was single it was inadequate for the traffic and the LSWR sought a route independent of the GWR. This was realised in 1890 over the Plymouth Devonport & South Western Junction Railway from Lydford to Devonport, henceforth a through station, and thence to the GW/LSW joint station at Plymouth North Road. The LSWR's own Plymouth Friary station was opened in 1891, access from North Road being over the GWR line as far as Lipson Junction, where this *up* LSWR Waterloo express is seen approaching the point where it joined the GWR *down* main line, an anomaly of GWR and LSWR workings that also existed at Exeter. The photograph, showing Adams 4-4-0 660 of 1895, is dated about 1910. In the left background can be seen the GWR Laira halt, opened for railmotor traffic in 1904, while behind the train is the GWR's Laira engine shed built in 1900 to replace the old Millbay shed.

Salisbury station about 1912 with two Drummond T9 4-4-0s on a Waterloo—Plymouth express. There were sixty-six engines of this famous class, built 1899-1901, and examples survived at Exmouth Junction, the LSWR's Exeter shed, until their final withdrawal in 1961. Below: one of the less successful Drummond 4-6-0s heads the 11am Waterloo—Torrington on the 1 in 80 climb of Honiton bank. In 1926 the SR named this train the Atlantic Coast Express and as such it ran until 1964, when express services between London and Exeter were concentrated on the former GWR route.

(Opposite above) The Southern Railway introduced a big programme of station rebuilding, examples in the West including Templecombe, Seaton, Exmouth and Exeter Queen Street, later known as Exeter Central. Seaton Junction, too, was rebuilt in 1937 providing extra centre tracks, and obviating reversal by Seaton branch trains. S15 Class 4-6-0 30823, on up freight, was of a design introduced in 1921 as a goods version of the King Arthur. The tall lattice post signal was of traditional LSWR design. The original station building was incorporated in the Seaton Junction rebuilding.

(Opposite below) Several engine sheds were rebuilt or modernised and at Ilfracombe a new shed was constructed soon after grouping.

Since both GWR and LSWR companies provided good restaurant car services, the Pullman did not prove successful in the West Country. The GWR's short lived trial was the Torbay Pullman in the summers of 1929 and 1930, after which it was withdrawn through lack of patronage. On the SR the Devon Belle was introduced in 1947, with portions to Plymouth and Ilfracombe. The train ran in the summer only, but in 1950 the Plymouth portion ceased and the train was withdrawn four years later. 4-6-2 34058 **Sir Frederick Pile** heads the down train near Crediton in August 1954. The train was unique in being scheduled to run non-stop between Waterloo and Sidmouth Junction. In practice, since there were no water troughs on the SR, it stopped to change engines at Wilton, west of Salisbury.

TRAFFIC CENTRES

Bristol Temple Meads, gateway to the West for GWR trains and indeed the only route from London until opening of the Castle Cary route in 1906. The early 1920s view opposite looking west shows the original GWR terminal station at right and the Bristol & Exeter building at top left. The station was rebuilt to provide additional platform accommodation in 1935.

The joint GWR/LSWR station at Weymouth in 1931. The overall roof of Brunel design was removed twenty years later. The centre part of the station with 263ft roof span was used by GWR trains, the smaller train sheds at left and right dealing with LSWR arrivals and departures respectively. Locomotives shown are GWR 'Bulldog' 4-4-0 3324 and SR 'T9' 4-4-0 730.

(Above) At Exeter St David's LSWR trains shared GWR tracks for just over a mile, as far as Cowley Bridge Junction, where GWR up trains headed east to Taunton and LSWR down trains west to Crediton. This 1906 view looking east shows the joint station at right, the goods station and avoiding lines used by through freight trains, and a nostalgic collection of engines at the engine shed.

(Opposite below) Exeter St David's in 1958 with 'Castle' 4-6-0 5069 **Isambard Kingdom Brunel** leaving with a Paddington—Kingswear train.

The LSWR station at Exeter Queen Street looking west. It was extensively rebuilt by the SR in 1927 and renamed Exeter Central six years later.

Newton Abbot is a market town and has always had important railway facilities. As junction for the Torbay line, main line expresses divided here for many years. More recently greater use has been made of Exeter as the interchange point. (Above) Newton Abbot station as it was between 1861 and 1927, when it was rebuilt to its present form. A 1903 view of **Earl of Devon** and **Cornubia** on the down Cornishman. (Below) South Devon Railway **Tiny,** built at Penryn in 1868, the last original broad gauge engine, is preserved on the down platform but may be placed in a museum.

(Above) The Sunday up Cornish Riviera leaves the joint station at Plymouth North Road in 1954. 5964 **Wolseley Hall** assists 6012 **King Edward VI** in readiness for the climb of the South Devon banks. Rebuilding of the station started in 1938, but all work ceased during the war and it was not completed until 1962.

(Below) Rebuilt Bulleid 4-6-2 34104 **Bere Alston** leaves Devonport with a Waterloo train. The overall roof originally provided here was destroyed by enemy action in 1941.

Par, junction of the branch to Newquay, was once a stopping place for all trains but nowadays the branch connection is made at Bodmin Road. The view above was at a time of severe flooding in the winter of 1903-4. The up main line train is headed by a 'Duke' class 4-4-0, an 0-6-0ST having brought in the Newquay train. Below, Truro, junction for Falmouth, prior to 1910 with down trains in charge of a '3521' class 4-4-0 and 'Bulldog' 4-4-0 3432 **River Yealm** (later renumbered 3380).

INCLINES

The hilly nature of parts of the West Country inevitably meant severe inclines particularly on the GWR main line between Newton Abbot and Plymouth, where two sharp climbs exist in either direction. Westbound trains have nearly three miles pull up Dainton bank followed after Totnes by the more protracted Rattery bank, while engines starting cold from Plymouth face the formidable 1 in 42 of Hemerdon bank and later Dainton bank, less severe in the eastbound direction. Working of the inclines was expensive in steam days since heavier passenger trains required an assistant engine, while loose-coupled freights needed banking.

6007 **King William III** nears Hemerdon summit with nine coaches, less than the 360 tons limit for such engines on Hemerdon bank, and on the westbound climb of Dainton. East of Newton Abbot a 'King' was allowed 530 tons, but the size of the Cornish Riviera which ran non-stop between Plymouth and Paddington was restricted to the number of coaches permitted on the South Devon banks.

Two little girls in their Sunday best clothes stand beside Rattery signal box in this picture of pre-1910 vintage. The Duke class 4-4-0 running light is thought to be 3321 **Mercury,** later renumbered 3287. Most interesting feature is the old bridge rail surviving on the down line in the foreground, while the up line has been relaid with sleepers and bullhead rail. The 'Dukes' and later the 'Bulldogs' were much used as assistant engines as below where 3393 **Australia** pilots 4910 **Blaisdon Hall** on the second part of the up Cornish Riviera Limited near Gwinear Road in 1933.

Worst gradient on the LSWR was the three mile climb out of Ilfracombe, largely at 1 in 36, while in the reverse direction the five miles from Braunton to Mortehoe included substantial stretches at 1 in 40. Until the advent of the West Country class, the N Class 2-6-0s of SECR design were extensively used on former LSWR lines west of Salisbury. This Ilfracombe—Barnstaple train climbing the 1 in 36 out of Ilfracombe was headed by 2-6-0 A838 of this type, in the summer of 1929.

(Below) A general view of the bank with Drummond 0-4-4T coasting down towards Ilfracombe on a local train.

RAILWAY STRUCTURES

The distinguished engineer, Isambard Kingdom Brunel, left his mark on many of the lines associated with the GWR. Probably his best known work is the famous Royal Albert Bridge spanning the River Tamar at Saltash, here seen under construction. It was his last and greatest masterpiece for he died soon after its completion in 1859.

Brunel also designed the many timber viaducts throughout the system but probably best known in Cornwall, where there were no less than forty-eight of them. They became increasingly expensive to maintain and replacement of those on the main line began in 1871 and was completed fifty years later when that at Penzance was converted to a stone embankment. Attention was then turned to the nine on the Falmouth branch, which were replaced between 1923 and 1934, although others survived in South Wales for a few years longer.

(Above) A Falmouth branch train crosses Collegewood Viaduct in the 1890s. This was the last of the Cornish timber viaducts to be replaced, in July 1934. (Below) A remarkable view of Carnon viaduct taken from a Falmouth train on the newly opened replacement bridge, August 1933.

An unusual view of Meldon Viaduct, near Okehampton, on the LSWR line from Exeter to Plymouth. The six span viaduct is supported by metal piers, the tallest being 120ft. It is immediately adjacent to Meldon limestone quarry which once supplied the whole of the SR's track ballast needs and had an annual output of over 300,000 tons.

The fine Treffry viaduct was built in 1843 to enable horse drawn trains of china clay to cross the Luxulyan valley. Below track level water was carried to provide power to work the winding gear of an incline. The early railway was replaced in 1874 on opening of the present Par—Newquay line passing beneath it. The 1953 summer Saturday picture shows the 12.30pm Newquay—Paddington in charge of 4-6-0 5998 **Trevor Hall** and 2-6-0 6305.

Inevitably many West Country structures used locally hewn stone in their construction. (Above) Pensford viaduct on the GWR Bristol, Radstock and Frome branch. Nearly 1,000ft in length, the tallest arch is 95ft. The enthusiasts' special crossing it is headed by the distinguished 4-4-0 **City of Truro**, now preserved in Swindon Museum, assisted by 2-6-2 tank 5528. (Below) A stone built signal box at Wadebridge, with the signalman about to hand over the single line token for the line to Bodmin North. The lefthand line is the single line for trains to Boscarne Junction and Wenford Bridge, also used by GWR trains to Bodmin General.

This view of Totnes station between the wars shows its original train shed form as built in 1847. The train sheds have since been demolished as also has the tower for the atmospheric pumping station, the top of which can be seen above 0-6-0 pannier tank 2785 on a local goods. (Below) GWR stations serving towns of any importance in the West were originally provided with overall roofs, used also by the LSWR to a lesser extent. This view of Salisbury GWR shows how gloomy the interiors of such stations could be. The engine is 'Bulldog' 4-4-0 3329 **Mars**. Exeter St Thomas was the last main line survivor in this form, the roof having been removed in 1970, but Ashburton, terminus of the Dart Valley line, is still intact.

TRAINS IN TROUBLE

The Norton Fitzwarren accident of 11 November 1890 involved a narrow gauge goods train, piloted thus far by a broad gauge engine. The pilot came off here and, after shunting was completed, the goods crossed to the up main line to allow the passage of a down train. The signalman then forgot its presence and gave 'Line Clear' for an up liner special from Plymouth Docks to Paddington. The special, a broad gauge saddle tank, two bogie coaches and a van, had made the usual high speed descent of Wellington bank when it came into violent head-on collision with the goods, resulting in the death of ten passengers. Bristol & Exeter Railway 4-4-0ST 2051 never ran again, but the standard gauge Armstrong Goods 1100 survived until 1916.

Fifty years later, on 4 November 1940, the most recent serious accident in the west took place, also at Norton Fitzwarren. The Paddington—Penzance night sleeper normally used the down main line west of Taunton but that night it was running late and diverted to the relief line to allow a newspaper train to overtake it. Approaching Norton Fitzwarren the two trains drew level and only then, too late to remedy his mistake, did the passenger train driver realise that he had confused the main line signal as his own. Seconds later the train ran through open trap points, its first six coaches derailed. resulting in 28 deaths. The engine, 6028 **King George VI** landed in soft earth and was little damaged.

The derailment between Doublebois and Bodmin Road on 16 April 1895 involved 0-4-4 tanks 3521 and 3548, formerly broad gauge 'convertibles', traditional West Country engines. The track was said to have been spread by two similar engines working the down Cornishman earlier that day. This led to withdrawal from main line duties and eventual rebuilding as 4-4-0 tender engines. There was an interesting sequel three years later when a new LSWR Drummond M7 0-4-4T was derailed at speed near Tavistock. The Inspecting Officer again criticised the use of front-coupled tanks on express trains, after which the M7s became more familiar in the London area although many spent their later years on West Country branches.

The '3521' Class as first built were 0-4-2 saddle tanks. Standard gauge engines 3521-39 proved so unsteady as to be rebuilt to 0-4-4 side tanks, in which condition 3540 was first built. All but two of the 3541-60 batch were broad gauge 'convertibles', being altered directly after the 1892 gauge conversion. It is evident that there was a history of rough riding even before the Doublebois accident and the derailment of 3542 with a Falmouth branch train at Penryn, 1 November 1898, finally convinced the authorities of the need to rebuild the class from their front-coupled form.

On 18 November 1885 Adams 0-6-0 442 was derailed when working an Exeter—Plymouth passenger train on the mixed gauge line near Yelverton before the LSWR had its own route to Plymouth. The engine's rigid wheelbase was partly to blame and the class ceased to work main line passenger trains in the West, being in any case primarily intended for freight traffic.

Worst accident in the West took place at Salisbury in the small hours of 1 July 1906 when an up Ocean Liner Express failed to observe the speed limit through the station and the train was wrecked by derailment resulting in 30 deaths. This was at a time of intense competition between the GWR with ocean mails and the LSWR with passengers from Plymouth Docks, in the course of which the GWR 4-4-0 **City of Truro** achieved its legendary 102.3mph. Ironically, on the day of the accident the GWR opened its direct route to the West via Castle Cary. There was no more racing on the LSWR and in 1910 the rival companies came to terms and LSWR participation in the ocean liner traffic ceased.

By virtue of their position, West Country lines suffered less from dislocation by heavy snow than their counterparts in the north. Even so lines close to the mountain slopes of Dartmoor were affected in hard winters, notably of course the Princetown branch, where this '1901' class 0-6-0ST was recorded, possibly in the hard winter of 1891. In 1905 small 2-6-2 tanks took over branch working until closure fifty years later. At 1,400 feet above sea level Princetown was the highest railway station in England.

That part of the South Devon line beside the sea between Starcross and Teignmouth has always suffered from the effects of gales and high seas. Between 1903 and 1958 the Teign Valley line provided a useful alternative when the coast line was flooded. After nationalisation the SR line from Exeter to Plymouth was substituted, but that line too was closed in 1968 between Okehampton and Bere Alston exclusive. In February 1969 the coast line was again flooded and freight traffic diverted by the SR route for the last time, the line having since been lifted. 6981 **Marbury Hall** was recorded at Dawlish on a down empty stock train at a time of heavy seas, September 1963.

COASTAL AND HOLIDAY LINES

Surely West Country lines are best remembered by holidaymakers for there were few coastal resorts not served by the railway. Nowadays the reverse is the case for BR has found such lines unremunerative since traffic outside the summer months was often negligible.

(Above) The line skirting the Hayle Estuary from St Erth to St Ives opened in 1877. This early view of St Ives shows broad gauge track. (Below) First train at Swanage in 1885 with LSWR Beattie tank 209 in charge. Both lines survive at the time of writing.

1906 scene at Bude with LSWR Adams 0-4-4 tank 211 in charge of the branch train. In early SR days this engine was shipped to the Isle of Wight, where it survived to the end of steam in 1966, having outlived the Bude branch by a few months.

BR 2-6-2T 82025 heads an Exeter—Exmouth train approaching Exmouth in 1960. The line has fairly good residential traffic throughout the year and so still remains open.

The Lyme Regis branch was built as a light railway and opened by the LSWR in 1903. Its first engines were two small Stroudley 'Terriers' bought from the LBSCR, one of which is seen at Lyme Regis (above). The six-coupled wheelbase did not prove suitable on the sharp curves and after unsatisfactory use of Adams 0-4-4 tanks for a few years the Adams 4-4-2 tanks were introduced in 1913, with such success that they worked the line until 1961. (Below) 30584 tackles the 1 in 40 climb through Combpyne woods in 1960.

For many years the LSWR ran a West of England express out of Waterloo at 11am but it was not until 1926, in SR days, that it was given the name Atlantic Coast Express. This remarkable train, and its corresponding up working, had through coaches for Seaton, Sidmouth, Exmouth, Plymouth, Torrington, Ilfracombe, Bude and Padstow. 'West Country' class 4-6-2 34033 **Chard** heads the latter portion across Little Petherick Creek, near Padstow in 1962. The North Cornwall line to Padstow closed in 1966.

How many generations of holidaymakers have watched the expresses pass on the coastal stretches of Dawlish and Teignmouth? Above, in broad gauge days 4-2-2 **Timour** heads an up express out of Teignmouth in 1891, while below, a decade later a Dean 4-2-2 heads an up express formed of clerestory stock approaching Dawlish. This section of the line through the tunnels west of Dawlish was not doubled until 1905.

The line from Newton Abbot to Kingswear, serving Torquay, Paignton and the Brixham branch, used to have considerable traffic at summer weekends and, unlike many branches, could be used by the largest engines. The Churchward mixed traffic 2-8-0s were regular summer visitors and 4700 is seen near Goodrington on the down Torbay Express, 4 August 1951.

RURAL BRANCHES

In the nineteenth century, before the coming of the internal combustion engine, the condition of country roads often left much to be desired and so the rural railway prospered. Since many arrived late on the railway scene, stations were often some distance from the villages they served, hence their decline in the motor age.

The Princetown branch, which opened in 1883 and closed in 1956, was an example of a line that served places far removed from the road. 2-6-2 tank 4410 draws a train for Yelverton into Ingra Tor Halt, beside a long disused granite quarry. The line traverses the slopes of Dartmoor at two higher levels in this picture since it negotiated the climb to Princetown, 1,400ft above sea level, in spiral fashion.

Country station scenes soon after the turn of the century. (Above) The LSWR station at Ottery St Mary on the branch to Sidmouth, opened in 1874 and closed in 1967, with Adams 0-4-4T 182 in charge of a lengthy train. (Below) The GWR line from Plymouth to Tavistock was opened in 1859 and extended to Launceston six years later. In 1883 the Princetown branch opened, traffic initially leaving the Tavistock line at Horrabridge. It was nearly two years before Yelverton station was opened at the physical junction of the branch. It soon became a busy station as seen here with a '3521' class 4-4-0 entering on a Launceston—Plymouth train.

The Culm Valley line from Tiverton Junction to Hemyock, opened in 1876, was built as a light railway and worked accordingly by small tank engines. (Above) GWR 0-4-2T 1462 at the Hemyock terminus. Passenger traffic has been withdrawn but the line remains open for milk traffic. (Below). A 3rd class carriage of 1854 used on the branch in the 1880s; note that one oil lamp sufficed to light the three compartments.

(Opposite) The North Devon & Cornwall Junction Light Railway from Torrington to Halwill was not opened until 1925. For many years traffic was worked by former LBSCR Stroudley 0-6-0 tanks rebuilt with a radial trailing axle and in this form used exclusively in the West Country. SR 0-6-2T 2608 of this type heads a train near Torrington. Passenger traffic ceased in 1965 but the line from Torrington to Meeth survives for clay traffic.

Drummond T9 4-4-0 30719 pauses at Tower Hill on the borders of Devon and Cornwall with the 9.56am Okehampton—Padstow. The guard consults his watch, but the up Padstow portion of the Atlantic Coast Express, which crossed here, was running dead on time. Even though veteran engines were often used well into BR days, timekeeping and station working on SR lines in the West was usually exemplary.

In their day the Drummond T9s had the reputation of being the fastest engines on the LSWR main line and they played their part in the high speed running during the period of competition with the GWR for the Plymouth Ocean Liner traffic. The last survivors ended their days on the North Cornwall line and on the main line west of Exeter, including a regular duty on the up Plymouth portion of the 'Atlantic Coast Express' until their final withdrawal in 1961. BR Western Region took over the former LSWR lines in Devon and Cornwall in 1963 and few now survive.

'Bulldog' 4-4-0 3416 **John W. Wilson** stands at Swimbridge in 1935 with a Taunton—Barnstaple train. Stops at GWR stations sometimes tended to be protracted. There was always time for the porter to discuss his lettuces or border plants with the guard. There were day old chicks on trolleys for loading and parcels from faraway places to be unloaded. To the railway enthusiast this leisurely progress was part of the charm of travel on a GWR branch line but it must have been frustrating to those in a hurry.

The GWR 'Bulldogs' had 5ft 8in driving wheels compared with the 6ft 7in diameter of the LSWR T9s, hence they were better known as branch line engines and as such were very familiar in the west country. The Barnstaple branch was one of their strongholds for many years until once familiar engines such as **Chaffinch** and **Cormorant** were eventually replaced by Churchward 2-6-0s. The last 'Bulldogs' were withdrawn in 1951 and the line from Taunton to Barnstaple only outlived them by fifteen years.

PORTRAIT OF A LOCAL LINE

The delightful Looe branch replaced a canal and has a complicated history. From Moorswater to Looe the Liskeard & Looe Railway opened for freight in 1860, initially worked by contractor's engine. North of Moorswater ran the Liskeard & Caradon Railway, opened as far as Caradon copper mine in 1844 and to Cheesewring granite quarries two years later. This was horse worked until 1862, from which date the L&C worked both systems throughout. In 1901, with the L&C in financial difficulties, the position was reversed with the L&L taking charge, but eight years later the GWR started working both lines and absorbed the L&C, the L&L staying nominally independent until 1923.

The L&C was never authorised to carry passengers and the notice opposite disguises the fact that it charged the holders of 'free passes' for conveyance of their umbrellas or handbags!

Between Moorswater and Looe a passenger service began in 1879. This was diverted to a platform adjacent to Liskeard GWR station in 1901, after which Moorswater was closed. The picture below shows surviving stone blocks near Cheesewring that once carried the tracks of the L&C, a part of the line never steam operated. The Caradon line was the last part of the L&C to survive, being lifted in 1917.

LISKEARD & CARADON RAILWAY

NOTICE.

FREE PASSES. CONDITIONS ON WHICH ALONE PERSONS ARE PERMITTED TO TRAVEL BY THE TRAINS ON THIS RAILWAY

No Person is to travel by the trains without a pass. All passes are issued gratuitously, but solely on the conditions that they are to be used only by the persons in whose favour they are issued, and that the use of any free pass, or the fact of travelling gratuitously, over any part of the Railway of the Company, shall be taken as evidence of an agreement with the Directors that neither the Company, nor the Directors, or their servants are to be responsible for any injury or damage which may occur to any person travelling by a free pass through accident, delay, or otherwise, whether occasioned by any act or neglect of the Company, or its servants, or otherwise, or for loss of or damage to property however caused.

All passes are only available on the day for which issued, they must be exhibited when required, and be given up at the end of the journey, and the holder is subject to the Bye-laws and other General Regulations of the Company.

BY ORDER OF THE DIRECTORS

LISKEARD & CARADON RAILWAY

Caradon in charge of a Sunday School excursion to the Cheesewring, the passengers riding in open wagons. **Caradon,** built at Middlesbrough in 1862, was the line's first engine and survived until 1907.

Lady Margaret with a train for Moorswater standing in Looe station was the last engine built for the line, in 1902, and it survived on the GWR until 1948. Despite their antiquated appearance the three four-wheeled coaches were built 1878-89, the bogie saloon coach dating to 1901.

A group at Looe station in early GWR days with GWR 4-4-0 saddle tank 13 and GWR coaches. Opposite, a guard in L&L uniform stands beside an ex-Mersey Railway coach, and a view of 2-6-2 tank 4569 in the last years of steam. The Looe branch can be seen to advantage from the diesel railcar still serving it.

'Travelling' by Bernard Moore from
A Cornish Chorus

'Peckham Rye, Loughborough, Elephant, St Pauls,'
Every morning the porter bawls,
The train grinds out . . . and I gaze on lots
Of sad back gardens and chimney-pots,
Factory stacks and smoky haze
Showering smuts on the close-packed ways.
And the train jolts on and twists and crawls . . .
'Peckham Rye, Loughborough, Elephant, St Paul's.'

But trapped and prisoned as I may be,
I lift a latch and my thoughts go free,
And once again I am running down
On a winding track from a Cornish town,
And I dream the names of the stations through—
'Moorswater, Causeland, Sandplace, Looe.'

An ancient engine with puff nigh gone
Drags a couple of coaches on
Close where a stream runs all the way
Muttering music night and day;
There isn't a porter about at all
To spoil the peace with a raucous bawl,
But a kind old guard to see me through,
Give me a ticket, and take it too.
The line twists down through patches sweet
Of soft green pasture and waving wheat
And the stream spreads out to a river wide
Where ships creep up at the turn of tide,
Till a tangle of spars on a blue sky spun
Gives me the sign of the journey done,
And I stand contented on the quay,
And hear the surging song of the sea.

So runs the dreamlike journey through
'Moorswater, Causeland, Sandplace, Looe',
But every morning the porter bawls
'Peckham Rye, Loughborough, Elephant, St Paul's.'

INDEPENDENT RAILWAYS

The Plymouth, Devonport & South Western Junction Railway served two purposes. Its main line between Lydford, Bere Alston and Devonport gave the LSWR access to Plymouth independent of the GWR's Tavistock and Launceston line. Opened in 1890 it was leased to the LSWR and worked by that company, although nominally independent, until the 1923 grouping. The PDSWJR itself operated the branch from Bere Alston to Callington (Kelly Bray) built in 1908 and incorporating part of a former 3ft 6in gauge mineral line.

At Callington shed, above, two of the line's three engines, 0-6-2 tanks **Earl of Mount Edgcumbe** and **Lord St Levan**. (Below), Calstock Viaduct, with twelve 60ft spans over the River Tamar, incorporated a wagon hoist for conveyance of wagons to and from the quayside.

64

Best known of the minor lines in the South West was the narrow gauge Lynton & Barnstaple Railway opened in 1898. The line was worked by three Manning Wardle 2-6-2 tanks, **Yeo, Exe** and **Taw,** a similar engine, **Lew,** being provided in 1925. Odd man out was 2-4-2 tank **Lyn,** which reached the line two months after opening from the Baldwin Locomotive Works, Philadelphia, USA. (Above) **Taw** approaches Lynton Station in August 1935, shortly before the line closed. (Below) The American engine **Lyn** with a train bound for Lynton in early SR days. The L&B was an early victim of road competition.

The Weston, Clevedon & Portishead Light Railway opened in stages between 1897 and 1907. The Portishead extension so drained its resources that the line remained in financial difficulties until closure in 1940. **Weston,** a Manning Wardle 0-6-0ST, heads a train over the level crossing at Clevedon.

The Bideford, Westward Ho! & Appledore Railway had a short life as a roadside light railway. Opened from Bideford Quay to Northam in 1901 and extended to Appledore in 1908, it was closed nine years later when the government commandeered the track. (Below) One of the line's three 2-4-0Ts on a train at Bideford.

The West Somerset Mineral Railway, as its name implies, was built primarily to serve the iron ore industry in the Brendon Hills, but between 1865 and 1898 it also carried passengers from Watchet to Comberow, where the 0-6-0ST **Pontypool** and train were recorded at the foot of the cable-worked incline. With a slump in the iron ore industry the WSMR closed in 1898, but reopened 1907-10 for mineral traffic only.

SOMERSET & DORSET

The Somerset & Dorset railway originated in 1862 by amalgamation of the Somerset Central, whose line from Burnham-on-Sea met end on at Cole, near Bruton, with the Dorset Central line from Wimborne, as then not completed. The line was ambitious but impecunious. A northward extension to Bath, steeply graded and involving extensive engineering works proved so costly as to lose the company its independence. First approach was made to the GWR, but in 1876 a joint lease by the Midland Railway and LSWR was authorised and thus the Somerset & Dorset Joint Railway was born. Although providing a useful north to south connection, the line was expensive to work and unprofitable.

The dignified Georgian style Midland Railway station, opened in 1870 for MR trains from Bristol and shared by the S&D from 1874, is a finer building than its GWR counterpart of 1840. Since the 1966 closure of the S&D it has become a car park. The bridge outside the station carries the familiar heraldic wyvern of the MR.

For many years the line relied on 4-4-0s for main line passenger work. (Above) 16, built at Derby in 1891 and rebuilt with larger boiler twenty years later. The glory of the attractive Prussian Blue livery can be seen. (Below) A Manchester—Bournemouth express passing Broadstone with 1920-built 67 in charge. Although allowed to haul 200 tons over the 1 in 50 graded line across the Mendips, these 7ft 0in engines were replaced by standard 6ft 9in 4-4-0s when the LMS took over provision of motive power in 1930.

The SDJR crossed the GWR on the level at two places, at Wells over the branch from Witham to Yatton and as shown above at Highbridge over the Bristol—Taunton main line. Ex-MR 0-4-4 tank 1379, which replaced similar SDJ engines, heads a train from Burnham-on-Sea. (Below) Summit point of the main line was at Masbury where in BR days ex-SDJ 0-6-0 44558 and SR 4-6-2 34040 **Crewkerne** were recorded on a northbound express of eleven coaches.

The MR remained faithful to the 0-6-0 for goods traffic to the end of its independent existence, as had the SDJR until 1914, in which year Derby built six 2-8-0s to haul freight traffic over the heavily graded Mendip line. 53809, ex-SDJR 89, was one of five further 2-8-0s built in 1925 and is shunting a freight train from Bath at Evercreech Junction under control of one of the distinctive reversing arm signals. A similar engine, 53808, is preserved by the Somerset & Dorset Circle at Radstock. In BR days these engines were much used on passenger trains in the summer months.

The last SDJR 2-8-0s were withdrawn in 1964, followed two years later by closure of virtually the whole of the S&D line. The GWR lost its opportunity to gain control in 1876 and as its cost conscious successor, BR Western Region, pursued a comparatively ruthless policy with unremunerative lines the outcome was inevitable when it took over the S&D.

RAILWAYS SERVING INDUSTRY

Although not primarily industrial in nature the south western counties had some interesting industrial lines, only a few of which survive. Among these is the Penlee Quarries line at Newlyn, connecting the quarry with the harbour. Of 2ft gauge it is the most westerly railway in England. **Penlee,** built by Orenstein & Koppel about 1900, was used until 1946 and still survives at the quarry. It is one of several German-built locomotives to have worked in Cornwall.

Pentewan Harbour was opened in 1826, primarily for the shipment of clay from St Austell, to which it was connected by the Pentewan Railway three years later. Trains were gravity or horse worked until 1874, when **Pentewan,** a Manning Wardle 0-6-0 was delivered. It survived twelve years when it was replaced by a similar engine which had an equally short life. Silting of the harbour made it suitable only for small vessels and this 2ft 6in gauge line ceased operating in 1918 when track and rolling stock were requisitioned for war work.

The Redruth & Chasewater Railway, nine miles of 4ft gauge track, was authorised in 1824 and partly opened the following year, the second railway in Cornwall. It never reached the more usually spelt Chacewater owing to decline in the copper mining industry. Steam was introduced in 1854, with two Neilson built 0-4-2 tanks, followed by a similar engine five years later. **Spitfire,** the later engine, was in this derailment at Devoran in 1899. All three survived until 1915 when the line closed.

The 3ft gauge line from Torrington to the North Devon Clay Co's works at Peter's Marland opened in 1880, in which year this Black Hawthorn 0-6-0ST was built. It is hauling a workmen's train across the River Torridge timber viaduct at Torrington. Workmen were conveyed in enclosed wagons and two old London horse tramcars. The viaduct was used until 1925 when the line was converted to standard gauge and extended to Halwill Junction on the North Cornwall line, as part of a light railway, the engineer of which was Colonel H. F. Stephens. It was always worked by the SR.

Another early line was the Lee Moor Tramway of 4ft 6in gauge dating back to 1858, but which followed part of the course of the 1823 Plymouth & Dartmoor Railway. Horse drawn trains carrying china clay continued to work down to Sutton Harbour, crossing the GWR main line on the level at Laira Junction, until 1960, by which time only part of the line survived. Two horses haul a return load of empties past Laira Yard, above, while below at the quarry is seen one of the two Bristol-built Peckett saddle tanks of 1899 used at that end of the line.

The Isle of Purbeck had two lines serving clay mines, of which the 2ft 8in line of Pike Bros was the best known and the most extensive. Based on Furzebrook, its principal branches were to Povington Mine, via Creech, and to Ridge Wharf on the Wareham river. Opened in 1866 it was steam worked until closure in 1956, although the Ridge branch closed when the area was commandeered in 1940. The locomotive **Secundus,** built at Birmingham in 1874, survives in a museum in that city. The 1911 view below shows a special train conveying members of the English Ceramic Society, when 1886 Manning Wardle tank **Tertius** provided motive power.

The second line, opposite, was that of B. Fayle & Co, of which the Middlebere Plateway dated back to 1806. In 1868 a new line was built from clay workings at Newtown to Goathorn Harbour and a steam engine was supplied by Stephen Lewin of Poole, its 3ft 9in gauge conforming with the plateway. In 1905 this line was extended to Norden, near Corfe Castle, making the old plateway redundant. In 1948 the Norden lines were converted to 2ft gauge and after 1953 were wholly diesel worked until closure in 1970.

The clay weathering beds at Norden in the 1890s with a horse drawn train crossing the LSWR Swanage branch opened in 1885. Below, the Lewin engine of 1868, which must have been delivered from Poole to Goathorn by barge. It survived until 1948.

FREIGHT TRAFFIC

The heavy industries, copper and tin mining and granite quarrying, were already in decline before the coming of railways and so freight traffic originating in the West consisted largely of perishable traffic such as fish, flowers, vegetables or milk, and the surviving mineral products, china clay from Cornwall, ball clay from Devon or Dorset, coal from Somerset. Broccoli traffic came from west Cornwall, including the Helston branch on which 4552 was recorded in 1960.

Below, 4-4-0 3291 **Tregenna** with an inspection special prior to opening of Drump Lane Goods station, Redruth, in 1913, recalling the days when every town had its freight depot, every station a siding. Nowadays goods traffic is increasingly concentrated on large centres and distributed by road.

For many years milk was carried in ten gallon churns conveyed to the railway stations by road transport as in the 1928 view above of Highbridge GWR station. The SDJ station overbridge can be seen in the background. Note, too, the once traditional pillbox hat of the GWR Stationmaster. In the 1930s glass lined tank wagons were introduced to convey the milk in bulk, each tank containing up to 3,000 gallons. (Below) 6801 **Aylburton Grange** passes Menheniot with a Penzance—Kensington milk train, 1956.

Cornish china clay traffic largely originates in the St Austell and St Blazey areas. Above, an early scene at the Cornwall Minerals Railway station of St Blazey, with a CMR six coupled engine at left. The station opened in 1874. (Below) SR Beattie tank 3314 in Pencarrow Woods on the 1834 branch of the Bodmin & Wadebridge Railway, with a train bound for Wenford Bridge, an important clay centre still served by rail.

Both GWR and SR companies favoured the use of mixed traffic 2-6-0s for much of their freight working. Above Churchward 2-6-0 6363 heads west at Fairwood Junction, Westbury, the 1933 avoiding line curving away to the right. Below SR 'N' Class 2-6-0 31849 hauls a load of china clay on the climb from Boscarne Junction to Bodmin General, with another 2-6-0 banking in the rear. Both are 1964 views.

HARBOURS AND SHIPPING

In the area encompassed by this volume the large expanse of coastline is well served by harbours, many of which had rail connections. The LSWR concentrated its passenger vessels at Southampton but between 1904 and 1910 it competed with the GWR for the Plymouth ocean liner traffic. It also helped develop the port facilities at Padstow and Fremington. The GWR had a greater interest in Plymouth Docks and from 1889 operated the Channel Islands steamship services from Weymouth. Fowey Harbour was substantially developed for china clay shipments and has only recently passed out of railway ownership.

An early view of Watchet Harbour, served by a branch from Taunton opened in 1862. The 4-4-0 saddle tank is Bristol & Exeter Railway 74, built in 1867, which became GWR 2047 in 1876 and survived until the end of the broad gauge.

The Millbay Docks at Plymouth became GWR property when the South Devon Railway was absorbed in 1876. The earliest Plymouth Docks ocean liner tender was built in 1873. (Above) The **Sir Francis Drake** was one of the tenders used between 1908 and 1947. (Below) Although the name Dartmouth appeared on the destination boards of Paddington expresses, the station there was served by steamer from Kingswear across the river. **The Mew** was the vessel regularly employed from 1908 to 1955.

The Channel Islands service from Weymouth originated long before the railway reached the town, in 1857. In that year the LSWR, which traditionally operated its marine services from Southampton, began a service from Weymouth. This proved short lived, being withdrawn in 1859, but it caused the GWR to take an interest in a local steam packet company which also commenced operations in 1857. Neither the harbour facilities nor the train service showed any improvement until 1889 when the GWR took over the local company and set the pattern that was to be followed for the next sixty years. Unlike Southampton, which was railway owned, Weymouth Harbour has always been municipally owned and improvements made have been in conjunction with the local authority.

Weymouth Harbour in 1911 with the **Ibex,** built at Birkenhead twenty years earlier. It was on the rocks twice, in 1897 off Jersey and three years later off Guernsey, but nevertheless survived until 1925. This vessel was the one member of the Channel Islands fleet to maintain the service in World War I, the others being engaged on war work.

In 1925 the **St Julien** and **St Helier** were built, the first new vessels for the Weymouth route since 1897. Both vessels were commandeered for war service and played a conspicuous part in the Dunkirk evacuation. The **St Helier** survived until 1960 and **St Julien**, approaching Weymouth Harbour in this 1929 view, followed it to Belgian shipbreakers in 1961.

Note the 'Channel Island Boat Express' roofboards on the coaches, a familiar feature until the latter part of 1959 when the Paddington service ceased. BR Southern Region had assumed responsibility for Weymouth soon after nationalisation and it was a logical step for the boat train service eventually to be diverted to Waterloo. In 1961, coinciding with the introduction of two new vessels, the train service was improved and Channel Islands sailings from Southampton ceased. Nowadays the short sea route from Weymouth to the Channel Islands is holding its own so far as passenger traffic is concerned but the future of the declining freight traffic is obscure.

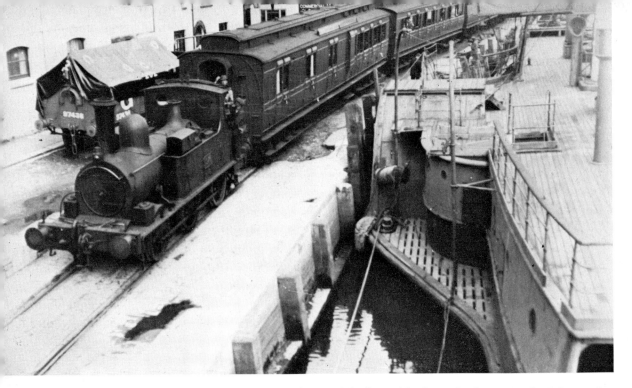

The Weymouth Harbour Tramway runs from a junction with the main line near the joint station through the streets abutting on to the quay. 1376 was one of two B&ER 0-6-0 tanks intended for the Hemyock line but which spent most of their lives hauling boat expresses and freight trains at snail's pace over the tramway.

The Poole Quay Tramway was a similar line in use from 1874 to 1960 for freight traffic only. Ex-LSWR 0-4-0T 30093 passes the old Customs House.

WEST COUNTRY LOCOMOTIVES

This photograph taken at Dorchester in 1860 by Major John Warry must be one of the earliest West Country railway photographs. The LSWR 2-2-2 **Vesta** was one of nine built by Sharp Brothers in 1838 and much used on the Southampton and Dorchester line. Two of these, together with a six-coupled goods engine, hauled the first cheap day excursion from Dorchester to Southampton on 4 August 1849, the load consisting of no less than twenty-one carriages and forty-nine open wagons.

Between 1873 and 1880 Beyer Peacock built eight small 0-6-0s ordered by W. G. Beattie for use on the steeply graded Ilfracombe extension. The climb starts almost at the end of Ilfracombe station and this view of 283 in charge of a Barnstaple train shows the contrast in grade between the branch, and the carriage sidings on the level. The LSWR withdrew them by 1913 but six were sold for use on Colonel Stephen's light railways in Kent and Shropshire.

Both Adams and Drummond built express 4-4-0s for the LSWR, those used between London and Salisbury having 7ft 1in coupled wheels, and those used west of Salisbury having a diameter six inches less. Of the latter type the Adams '460' class of 1884 were familiar West Country engines. In SR livery 0473 was recorded on a freight train at Barnstaple Junction in 1927, when fitted with a Drummond boiler.

The Bristol & Exeter Railway and the South Devon Railway were great users of 4-4-0 saddle tanks for passenger work and many survived until the end of the broad gauge in 1892. Until absorbed by the GWR in 1876, SDR engines were distinguished only by their names. The example above, **Sol,** carrying GWR No 2125, was built at Bristol by The Avonside Engine Co in 1866.

(Below) B&ER 42, one of eight 9ft single driver tanks built for main line express work 1853-4. No 42 was recorded at Bristol in 1865 showing evidence of damage after a mishap near Weston.

(Above) Until the end of steam on GWR branch lines the lively small 2-6-2 tanks were to be encountered. The eleven engines of the 44xx class were built 1904-6, to be followed by no less than 175 engines of the 45xx class, built between 1906 and 1929. 3104, later 4404, was recorded at South Brent when new, being used on the Kingsbridge branch. The cast-iron 'S' plate on the signal box was a means of drawing the lineman's attention to any failure of the signalling equipment.

(Opposite below) 0-6-0ST 1397, recorded at Taunton 1922, was an 1883 rebuild of a Cornwall Minerals Railway 0-6-0T of 1873, one of nine similar machines not only familiar West Country engines in their own right but also because they were the basis for the design of the 1910 built '1361' class, of which 1363 survives, preserved at Bodmin by the Great Western Society.

The 'Duke' class 4-4-0s were built 1895-9, being intended primarily for work on the main line west of Exeter, their 5ft 8in wheels being well suited to the gradients encountered. In Cornwall they replaced the '3521' class 4-4-0s rebuilt from 0-4-4 tanks, but in the present century they were in turn replaced on main line work by 'Bulldog' 4-4-0s and later by Churchward 2-6-0s and 4-6-0s. 3273 **Armorel** was recorded on the turntable beside Penzance station. Originally installed for smaller engines, note the turntable extension rails fitted to accommodate tender engines.

This 1953 view at Okehampton shed contrasts two types long associated with the West. At left is 'West Country' 4-6-2 34017 **Ilfracombe,** of 1945 vintage, and at right 1899-built Drummond T9 4-4-0 30712. There were 110 of the Bulleid light 'Pacifics', sixty-eight of which carried West Country names. Several were ceremonially named by local dignitaries, as, for example, 21C142 **Dorchester,** later 34042, shown below.

RAIL AND ROAD MOTORS

The LSWR was the pioneer in developing the steam railmotor, small self-contained vehicles initially designed as an economical answer to increasing electric tramway competition. The first two cars were placed on the LSWR/LBSCR joint service from Fratton to East Southsea in June 1903. The GWR was quick to follow suit and its first car entered service between Stonehouse and Chalford four months later. In addition to the two joint railmotors the LSWR had fifteen such vehicles, while by 1908 the GWR had no less than ninety-nine in service. Thereafter the lack of flexibility of such vehicles proved their downfall. Where their introduction provided frequent trains and cheap fares they generated more traffic than they could manage, even with a trailer attached, whilst stabling at locomotive sheds led to cleaning problems with the coach portion. They ended their days on sparsely used branch lines, the last LSWR car going in 1919, while the GWR retained some as late as 1935.

First LSWR railmotor service in the South West was that between Plymouth and Turnchapel, commenced in August 1904. Car 2 was recorded at Plymouth Friary. They were later used between Plymouth and St Budeaux; Exeter and Topsham; Bodmin, Wadebridge and Padstow and briefly on the joint line from Weymouth to Portland.

GWR steam railmotors were much used throughout the West, and some specially large cars worked the Plymouth suburban services. Busy scene at Dorchester GWR in 1908 with large capacity car 46 in the foreground. The destination board reads 'Came Bridge, Upwey Wishing Well, Upwey, Radipole and Weymouth', a service on which railmotors were introduced on 1 June 1905. Prior to this Upwey had been the only intermediate station—the coming of railmotors brought the opening of many small halt platforms.

The GWR was an early user of the diesel railcar and built thirty-eight such vehicles between 1934 and 1942. These often replaced railmotor trains, as was the case with Car 20, seen entering Maiden Newton with a Yeovil—Weymouth train in 1952.

From the steam railmotor was developed the railmotor train, making use of existing engines fitted for push and pull working, coupled to suitable trailers having an end driving compartment used when the engine was propelling. The GWR made extensive use of 0-6-0 and 0-4-2 tanks for such services. 0-6-0PT 1271 enters Plymouth North Road with a Yealmpton—Plymouth Millbay train in 1925.

The LSWR, and later the SR, mainly used 0-4-4 tanks of Adams or Drummond design for motor train work. M7 0-4-4T 30055 pauses at Colyton with a Seaton train. The engine is propelling the two coaches, hence the tail lamp.

Credit is usually given to the GWR for being the first English railway company to introduce motor buses, but in fact it rightly belongs to the Lynton & Barnstaple Railway, which from April 1903 introduced petrol buses between Blackmoor station and Ilfracombe. North Devon was not then ready for such revolutionary ideas and a successful prosecution for having exceeded the 8mph speed limit caused the L&B chairman to dispose of the buses to the GWR. These two 16hp Milnes-Daimlers inaugurated the GWR Road Motor Department and were set to work between Helston and The Lizard in August 1903. From this modest beginning the GWR built up the largest of all railway owned bus fleets, operating over 300 vehicles. As early as the end of 1904 the GWR's thirty-six motor buses made it the largest operator in the country even exceeding the number of such vehicles in London. Between 1928 and 1933 the GWR buses were gradually split up among various bus companies, with whom the railway concluded financial agreements.

GWR Car No 1 outside Helston station in 1903 soon after inauguration of the service to The Lizard. At this time registration plates for motor vehicles had not been introduced. GWR policy was to convert superseded buses into lorries and No 1 still survived in this form at Slough in 1919.

The first GWR double-deckers were introduced between Penzance and Newlyn in 1904, also Milnes-Daimler vehicles. A similar vehicle is seen at Weymouth on the Radipole-Wyke Regis service introduced in 1905. This later became a joint service with the LSWR and was the last GWR service to operate, being taken over by Southern National from 1 January 1934. As Car No 58 in the GWR fleet list this bus was still in service at Saltash in 1917, but later became a lorry.

Only LSWR omnibus service in the West was its route to Chagford, initially in 1904 from Exeter but later from Yeoford Junction. The service lasted 20 years and apart from joint services was the longest lived LSWR omnibus operation. At Chagford two of the company's four Clarkson steam buses were recorded. They proved unreliable and it was said of them that they did a higher mileage running between Exeter and Exmouth Junction for repair than over the 21 mile route to Chagford!

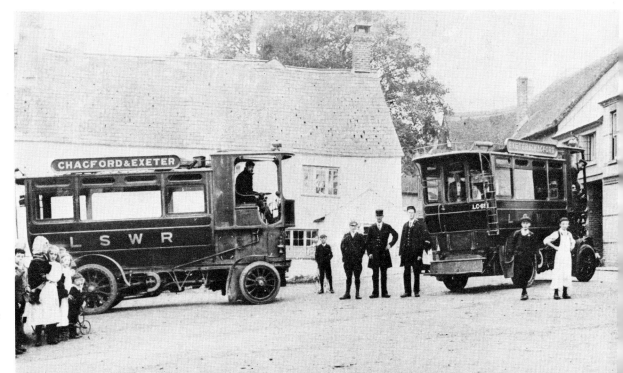

THE CONTRACTING RAILWAY

By its very nature, in the absence of many large centres of population, the West Country has seen a steady withdrawal of railway facilities, branch line closures having gained impetus long before publication of the 1963 Beeching Report. In the case of rural branches the last lines opened were usually the first to close.

Although well situated in the town centre, Yeovil Town ex-LSWR station closed as a result of the rationalisation of facilities. The Salisbury—Exeter main line by-passed Yeovil, but a connection, long removed, enabled trains from Salisbury to reach Hendford, the 1853 terminus of the Bristol & Exeter Railway branch from Taunton. Yeovil Junction station opened 1 June 1860 and Yeovil Town exactly a year later. The view above shows it in its early years.

The contrasting scene in 1967, the only line surviving being the connection to the Wilts, Somerset & Weymouth Railway station at Yeovil Pen Mill, still served by passenger trains between Westbury and Weymouth. The Taunton line closed in 1964, but a handful of trains ran between Town and Pen Mill for a year longer, while the passenger service to Yeovil Junction survived until 1966. Hendford Goods remained open until 1967. The Town—Pen Mill connection, latterly used only for access to the loco depot, closed in 1968.

Chard's first station was Chard Road, on the 1860 Salisbury—Exeter line, renamed Chard Junction in 1872, nine years after the opening of a three mile branch to Chard Town, LSWR. In 1866 the Bristol & Exeter Railway opened a branch from Taunton to Chard Joint station, later Chard Central, half-a-mile beyond the Chard Town terminus, which lost its passenger service at the end of 1916. This 1962 picture shows a train about to leave Chard Central for Chard Junction. The grass-grown platform at left conceals the former bay used by LSWR trains, and at right is the GWR engine shed, roofless and long disused. Passenger services ceased in 1962.

The little known LSWR station at Chard as it was in 1962.

The contrasting scene at Chard Central in 1966, when it survived as a private siding only. Goods traffic north of this point ceased in 1964, from which year also the line from Chard Junction was restricted to private siding traffic. The freight depot a Chard Town LSWR survived until April 1966—the passenger station, used as a sack store after its closure fifty years earlier, was gutted by fire in 1968. In May 1966 the branch closed altogether, although as twelve months' notice of closure of a private siding had to be given traffic was conveyed by road to Taunton Concentration Depot. The agreement lapsed in March 1967, ten months after the last train had run.

The nine mile South Devon Railway branch from Totnes to Ashburton opened in 1872. The passenger service was withdrawn in 1958 and goods traffic ceased four years later. (Above) Ashburton in 1920 with GWR '517' Class 0-4-2 tank on the branch train. (Below) The station in 1964, forlorn and neglected. It was later restored by the Dart Valley Light Railway Ltd which operates a summer service between Buckfastleigh and Totnes Riverside, a platform outside BR limits. The line's future is obscure as that part between Ashburton and Buckfastleigh is required for road improvements. Ashburton terminus, the last GWR overall roof station, saw its last train in October 1971.

MODERNISATION

The Western Region's first diesel express locomotive was delivered in 1958, and by the end of that year with a dozen in service and some initial teething troubles overcome, the Cornish Riviera and other Paddington—Penzance trains were diesel hauled. More recently, the WR's wisdom in choosing hydraulic transmission has been questioned, all other regions of BR using diesel-electric locomotives. Indeed, many are now on WR and a number of diesel-hydraulics have been condemned after a short life. Steam facilities were withdrawn from Cornish depots in 1962, but because of poor diesel reliability it was not until 1964 that steam haulage ceased west of Taunton.

This 1961 view shows 'Warship' Class D824 **Highflyer** passing Laira Junction. In the foreground part of the former Lee Moor Tramway crossing is to be seen. In the distance at left the new diesel depot takes shape, part of the steam shed being used pending its completion.

At Newton Abbot the former steam locomotive factory was completely rebuilt internally to adapt it for diesel maintenance. The last steam locomotive was repaired there in July 1960 and within two years it was operational for the new motive power. A weathervane in the shape of an old broad gauge engine survives as a nostalgic reminder of the old regime.

This view of 2,700hp D1064 **Western Regent** and 2,200hp D826 **Jupiter** shows a 1970 freight development on the Cheddar Valley line. D826 stands with empty wagons on the single line branch, at Merehead, a point between the former Wanstrow and Cranmore stations. D1064 heads a limestone train for Fareham on a new three-quarters-of-a-mile line built by Foster Yeoman Ltd for quarry traffic, and would reverse at the junction. To obviate the engine run-round trains are now propelled from the quarry. The 2,700hp 'Western' class are mostly used on this traffic and also handle most of the West Country express passenger services.

Diesel multiple-units were introduced at Plymouth in 1960 and their use is now widespread. Initially they were used on the Saltash suburban service replacing steam railmotor trains. Opening of the Tamar road bridge in 1961 brought a drastic reduction in traffic and curtailment of services the following year. 4087 **Cardigan Castle** restarts an up express against the grade after a signal stop outside Saltash, September 1960. In the siding stands one of the suburban type diesel units used on the local service.

The introduction of diesel units was acclaimed as the most economic means of branch line working but in the west they arrived too late on the scene to stem the tide of branch closures. Some branches were never included in the dieselisation proposals and were steam worked to the last, even though diesel units were firmly entrenched in the area. Thus it was with the Helston branch and Plymouth—Tavistock—Launceston. In other cases, such as Taunton—Minehead, even the economies of diesel working failed to save the day. On some of the surviving branches a single unit diesel railcar is more than adequate for the traffic remaining.

A cross-country diesel multiple-unit approaches Exeter St Davids, having worked a stopping service from Kingswear, July 1963. Behind Exeter West Box at left is the 1 in 37 climb to the former LSWR/SR station at Exeter.

Pending delivery of cross-country units some suburban units were used on quite lengthy journeys such as stopping trains between Plymouth and Penzance, which in view of their lack of amenities did not prove a popular expedient.

The former SR lines in the west were not included in the WR's dieselisation plans but by the time WR assumed responsibility for them in 1963, there had been sufficient retrenchment in WR services to provide adequate diesel power for its extension to those SR lines that survived under the new regime.

Class '2' 1,100hp locomotive D6342 emerges from Pinnock Tunnel with a St Blazey—Fowey china clay train, 1963. This branch closed in 1968 when English China Clays took over the harbour, and part of the line has been adapted for road use by the company's clay lorries. The 1,100hp diesels were far from successful and none survive.

The new power signal box at Plymouth, completed in 1960, replaced six mechanical boxes and controlled five route miles. Although modern at the time the massive strides in signalling technology since then enable the new Bristol box to control 117 route miles. Both illustrations depict Plymouth.

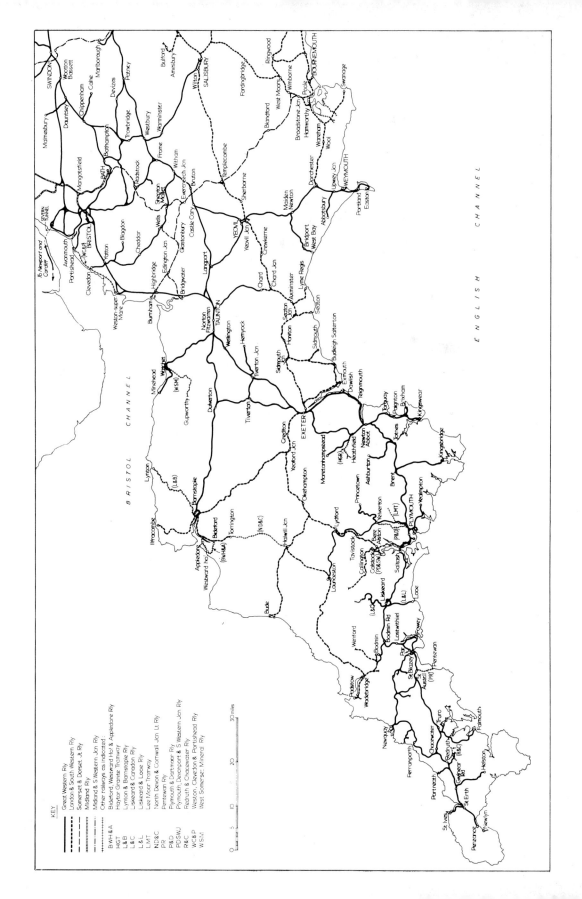

KEY

———————	Great Western Rly
– – – – –	London & South Western Rly
–·–·–·–	Somerset & Dorset Jt Rly
··········	Midland Rly
·+·+·+·	Midland & S Western Jcn Rly
	Other railways as indicated:
BWH&A	Bideford, Westward Ho! & Appledore Rly
HGT	Haytor Granite Tramway
L&B	Lynton & Barnstaple Rly
L&C	Liskeard & Caradon Rly
L&L	Liskeard & Looe Rly
LMT	Lee Moor Tramway
ND&C	North Devon & Cornwall Jcn Lt Rly
PR	Pentewan Rly
P&D	Plymouth & Dartmoor Rly
PDSWJ	Plymouth, Devonport & S Western Jcn Rly
R&C	Redruth & Chacewater Rly
WC&P	Weston, Clevedon & Portishead Rly
WSM	West Somerset Mineral Rly

0 5 10 20 30 miles

ACKNOWLEDGEMENTS

I should like to express my sincere gratitude to all those who have placed their photographic collections at my disposal. Specific acknowledgements for individual photographs reproduced in these pages are as follows:

Dr Ian C. Allan: 35, 36 (bottom), 39 (bottom). H. J. Ashman: 72. S. W. Baker: 66 (top), 70 (top). D. H. Ballantyne: 42. C. Batchelor: 108. Donovan E. H. Box: 49 (top), 57, 59. BR (Western Region): 8, 12, 13, 14 (top), 15, 16, 29, 30, 38, 56 (bottom), 61, 79, 83, 84, 85, 104 (top), 105, 109. C. L. Caddy, 99, 100, 101. F. H. Casbourn: 75, 88 (top). Bernard Chapman: 14 (bottom), 47 (bottom), 55 (top). J. M. Cummings Collection: 96. Dorset County Museum: 11 (bottom), 20, 87. M. W. Earley: 37. T. J. Edgington: 94 (bottom). A. G. Ellis Collection: 86. P. W. Gray: 10, 63 (bottom). A. Halls, courtesy M. W. Earley: 26 (bottom), 37 (bottom), 65 (bottom), 88 (bottom). M. D. Hardy Collection: 18, 21 (top), 52, 76, 77 (top), 91. H. H. Hole: 67. Holman Bros: 10. H. G. W. Household: 19 (bottom), 77 (bottom). B. L. Jackson Collection: 11 (top), 97 (top). W. H. C. Kelland: 69. L&GRP: 18 (bottom), 23 (top), 24, 31, 44, 48, 62 (centre), 63 (top), 66 (bottom), 68 (lower), 73 (bottom), 82, 90, 98. A. B. MacLeod Collection: 55 (bottom), 64 (top), 74, 94 (top). Rev A. H. Malan: 52 (top). Museum of British Transport: 22, 23 (bottom), 92 (bottom). S. C. Nash: 27, 51, 81 (bottom). T. W. Nicholls: 56 (top). Dr L. N. Owen: 41, 53. G. E. S. Parker: 60. Ivo Peters: 50 (bottom), 81 (top). W. Potter: 32 (bottom). P. J. T. Reed Collection: 15 (top), 16 (bottom), 22 (bottom), 32 (top), 34, 36 (top), 39 (top), 45, 62 (top/bottom), 64 (bottom), 73 (top), 78 (bottom), 80 (top), 89 (bottom), 90 (bottom), 93. Science Museum (Crown Copyright): 9. J. L. Smith Collection: 43, 47 (top), 80 (bottom), 97 (bottom), 102 (top). P. Q. Treloar: 78 (top). H. V. Tumility Collection: 25 (top), 46 (bottom), R. E. Vincent: 33, 92 (top). H. F. Wheeller: 65 (top).

Of the remaining illustrations those on pages 19 (top), 25 (bottom), 50 (top), 89 are from unidentified sources in the author's collection, while those on pages 8 (bottom), 21 (bottom), 26, 30 (bottom), 33 (bottom), 40, 42 (bottom), 49 (bottom), 54, 58, 68 (top), 70 (bottom), 71, 79 (bottom), 86 (bottom), 101 (top), 102 (bottom), 103, 104 (bottom), 106, 107 are the work of the author.   (

In addition I should mention the unfailing assistance of Mr N. W. Sprinks of BR Western Region Public Relations Department, coupled with Mr W. R. MacDonald (CCE Department, Paddington) and Mr C. Chilvers (CM&EE Department, Swindon), also Mr J. H. Scholes, Curator, Museum of British Transport, Clapham, and his photographic assistant, Mr J. G. Spence.

Mr J. M. Cummings kindly provided me with certain details of the GWR and LSWR omnibuses, while Mr R. Maund clarified certain obscure details of the declining years of the railway at Chard.

Last, but by no means least, my thanks are due as always to Christine, my wife, for her patience and encouragement at all stages during the production of this book.

INDEX